# THE WIND *of* SPOKEN WORDS

# THE WIND
## *of*
# SPOKEN
# WORDS

*poetry to engage your soul*

LANA LENSMAN

ISBN 979-8-9875062-2-6 (print)
ISBN 979-8-9875062-3-3 (e-book)

First Edition
Cover design by Holly Forrest

# CONTENTS

# OCTOBER

# NOVEMBER

# PREFACE

I have enjoyed an early morning practice of
stillness for many years. In the beginning, the quiet
was filled with thoughts streaming from my mind.
But as I became more comfortable with silence,
I began to hear the universal wisdom that speaks
beyond the mind.

On a new moon morning in March, I heard a
poem called The Blank Mind. This was the first
of many poems that came to me during the next
three cycles of the moon. This collection of poems
became the book, *The Face in the Night Sky.*

By the end of May, the poems stopped coming
in and my morning practice returned to normal.
Then on a quiet early morning in September,
I began hearing poetry again and this time it
continued for nine consecutive months, rendering
a total of 377 poems. *The Wind of Spoken Words*
includes the poems transcribed from September
through November.

I do not view these poems as my creation. My
ability to hear wisdom in the silence is what I take
credit for, not the wisdom itself. The words

contained in these books, spoken in poetic form,
originate from a higher source far beyond my
mind's capacity to comprehend.

I took great care to not interfere with the pure
vibration of this literary creation. No edits were
made to constrain the poems to abide by the
formal rules of poetry. The poems were preserved
in the order they were received and with the line
spacing in which they were heard.

During the initial weeks of hearing poetry, I also
received the title of the first book and the number
of poems it would contain. I had a dream about
a mandala and woke up and drew an image of it.
This would be the way readers would engage with
the poems.

Even though it has been several months since
I first began hearing poetry, I continue to be
guided through the process. I spend my time now,
reading the poems and preparing the next book for
publication.

*Close your eyes. Point your finger and touch the mandala.*
*Open your eyes to see the poem that wants to engage with you.*
*Each poem offers an entry point into the soul journey.*
*It will guide you inward, a slow spiral into the heart of creation.*
*Replicating nature's way, the energy of the mandala wants to*
*find center and then return, moving outward into life expression.*

Empty Seconds The Deeper Story The Sacrifice Deep Connection Absorption Downpour Nothing Wrong This Busy World Soul and Body Ashes Solid Next Step Purity Extinguished Vacancy Deep Down Knowing Two Views Two Way The New Way Soul Direction Savored Left Behind Plant New Seeds Smooth Push and Pull Emptiness Daily Spin Saturated Orbit of Nothing Together In Motion Earth Walk Soul Mind's Way Streaming Fog's Illusion Clear Water Desire Your Words The Origin of You The Thread Lost Words Next Step Solid Soul's Seed Seed Turned Around Love Relationship Evolved Soul Depth Poetry New Seeds Invisible Soul's Voice Sound to Silence Not My Story Shine Bright Broken Words Seen Small Hunts Your Story You and Soul Light and Joy The Flame Water Being Within Reach The Web Lost and Found Vast Space Carry Me Me

# INTRODUCTION

Enter The Wind of Spoken Words with a
desire to know your soul.

In the silence, universal wisdom awaits you.
As you quiet your mind, you become open to
the vast possibilities of creation. You move out
of a narrow channel of thinking into a more
expansive state of being.

Using the mandala, each poem becomes the
doorway into another world, a world that lives
within you. Inside this sacred space you can
create your present reality. And when fueled by
your heart's desire, you can bring your soul's
voice out from the silence.

# SEPTEMBER

## empty seconds

Tick tock, tick tock
one second gone
and then another.

Each second
an empty vessel
awaiting intention
yearning for purpose.

Empty seconds
become empty minutes
then empty hours
and soon, wasted days.

Seconds left neglected
and unmemorable,
result in time
without meaning.

## the deeper story

A vision appears
in a puff of smoke
quick with insight
fast to disburse

I track the scent
of this latest clue
entering the realm
of pending time

where guidance
streams down
like pouring rain,
gathering in pools
over matter

and dreams
cast characters
in eternal landscapes,
weaving together
the deeper story.

Mind is the storyteller.
Body moves these stories into reality.
Consciousness displays
the intricate art of its creator.

## the sacrifice

Step into her world
but be prepared
to give generously.

As she is done with Takers,
those who consider only their needs
and become filled up
on what they can get from her.

She is done with The Sacrifice,
offering too much of herself
or giving her life away.

Step into her world
but be prepared to be kind,
to care about someone
other than yourself.

As she is ready to receive
the love and support
she deserves.

## deep connection

I cherish the world I have created
the hours spent shaping my life
the contribution I have made to Love

I cherish the person I have become
a soul in union with body
energy contained and clear
a greater view of Life

My world thrives on
the daily pursuit of harmony
the integration of wisdom
the fulfillment of emptiness

It rotates
within an atmosphere
of deep connection

## *absorption*

Idling on empty,
waiting to be filled with substance
that penetrates dark matter
until it expands into Light.

Soul's river swells
flowing over
slowly seeping into
empty spaces.

Absorption
becomes solid
knowing
sure being
Full.

# *downpour*

All at once
a stream of insight
flows down
within my
being

Drenched,
I slowly absorb
its potency
into the dense
layers

In this downpour,
particles swirl and swell
until all settles
into
wisdom

Integration leads
alignment follows,
Body and Soul
are
One

## *nothing wrong*

Leave behind
the lens of perfection
and take in the view
of Nothing Wrong.

Find acceptance
in what you see
whether it fills or drains,
it's reality.

You can't change a story
without soul purpose.
No use resisting
what can't be undone.

Look within,
find a deeper truth,
a way of seeing
that lightens you.

## *this busy world*

Humans, racing by
with narrow vision
quickened pulse
lost in thought
void of body
on to the next thing
no time to pause
look closely
breathe deeply

Each experience
on the surface

Each interaction
barely reached

Each accomplishment
a fleeting reward

Observing
this busy world,
I feel Earth's loneliness.

## ashes

What's in the past
serves no purpose
provides no fuel.

Once seen and felt
once understood,
leave it behind you.

The past transformed
into a pile of ash
returns to earth.

Memories remain,
attachment is gone.

*solid*

Strength is solid
Weakness is permeable

Containment is strength
Carelessness is weakness

Wisdom
is acquired
through strength

Alignment
relies upon
containment

Aligned wisdom
is Solid.

*next step*

Step towards
what sparkles
attracts your eyes
lightens your body.

Step away from
what arises from shadows
in murky vision
and heavy heart.

Step into
The New World.

## *purity*

Thoughts resonate
with feelings

Words align
with action

Clear energy
finds its match

Body and Soul
are One

Purity
is your
life purpose.

## *extinguished*

If the smoke of self-doubt
evades your grasp
it will billow into an atmosphere
of uncertainty.

Extinguish the sparks of confusion
that tell you,
you aren't good enough
or it can't be done.

Douse the flames of fear
with Truth
until reality
can be touched.

Let Soul's fire
ignite within you
until all you can see
is the pure flame of Yes.

## vacancy

People line up
filled with admiration
for what I have achieved

I feel a vacancy,
I can't absorb what they see.

The evidence is apparent
the proof is secure

I can't feel it, I can't touch it
absorption remains obscure.

How can I soak in reality
and breathe in life's truth
when a part of me denies the good
and diminishes the proof?

I will bathe
in the stillness of me,
until silence
erases all discrepancy.

## *daily spin*

In the turning world
from deep within,
Soul moves you forward
in the most mysterious ways.

An invitation is extended
to participate
in this daily spin.

If you say "Yes,"
you will enhance
your soul evolution.

*emptiness*

Your past,
a pile of ashes
blown by the wind

Memories
seek to be held
but find no comfort

The rooms are bare
the house is empty
your old identity
has moved on

While your eyes
see the same view,
the same feelings
no longer exist

The flame can't ignite

You are left sitting with
the discomfort of emptiness,
hoping that in time
the essence of you will be felt

## *smooth*

Silence is my partner

Stillness,
a vehicle for movement

I listen
I dialogue
I feel

I breathe with Soul

Space is filled,
it's smooth

The world
waits for us

# *push and pull*

Within your body,
the magnetic force of fear
keeps you apart

while the compelling
strength of Soul
brings you together.

This push and pull
drains heart's reservoir
until it is bone dry.

Mind's strategies
attempt to sustain walls
create the distance.

Your awareness
sees the cracks
and destabilizes its existence.

# OCTOBER

## *saturated*

Soaking in
the softness of silence
I am slowly saturated
with soul's sweet song

I settle into
the serenity of solid
the sustenance of smooth
the seduction of stillness

Shhhh,
I hear the sound
of Spirit speaking

## orbit of nothing

The ticking clock
pulls me towards
Doing

Stillness
draws me into
Being

I feel the minutes
fall one by one
into the void.

In the orbit of nothing
zero has value
it's worth its weight

Dense matter absorbs
the air of Soul
while the harmony
of everything ignites.

# *together*

Motion flows out
breathes
then returns to center

The ebb and flow
of Together
is never far apart

Life's tide draws near
then retreats
in fluid rhythm

We ride the same wave

The same direction
the same desire
we touch Together

## *in motion*

Energy has a lifecycle,
its movement
can only be hindered
for so long.

Broken fragments
stored away
chisel steadily
until they are freed.

Movie clips
deeply buried
play at slow speed
until they are seen.

Without expression,
energy pressures
breath and heart
until its composure
falls apart.

Soon, what's in motion
floods the earth
drenching life
inviting birth.

## *earth walk*

I walk in river's flow
with the mountain
at my back

Wind blows through
while fire transforms
the excess

I sink into
the embrace of
earth's density.

## soul and body

What I think
What I feel
What I say
What I do

How is my soul in motion
with what I speak
and how I move?

What I choose
What I allow
What I receive
What I give

How is my body aligned
in the silence
of soul intention?

## the thread

When it comes to you
gently pick it up
hold it in your hand

The thread
is the beginning
of the path to the end.

Follow where it leads
don't let it go,
it is continuity in motion
the lifeline to your soul.

If you hold too tightly
or allow too much slack,
you will lose the balance
and the return will come back.

## *lost words*

Floating on air,
lost words
travel without purpose

They rise
then fall
onto the shallow surface.

Sometimes,
they're delivered
with great force of wind

with intention
to trample
any motion within.

Lost words
arrive as strangers
looking for a home

I would rather
leave an open space
with room for the unknown.

## deep down

Enter the sacred well
where present reality
reaches its depth

Float within the dark
until clouded water
rises clear

Deep down
the debris left dry
is touchable

Smooth its rough edges.

# *knowing*

Belief
follows a question,
Knowing
is before the answer.

Doubt
feeds belief,
Knowing
has already been fed.

Belief
proves nothing,
Knowing
needs no proof.

Within zero
belief is non-existent,
Knowing
is its breath.

*savored*

A whole bar of chocolate
devoured all at once
consumed in a frenzy
easily forgotten.

*or*

Consciously consumed
one small piece at a time
each taste experienced
fully savored.

## left behind

Mind rushes forward
into the vast space
seeking what's next

Ahead of time
eager to be fed
grasping for more.

When mind directs
life's future,
the Unseen
is left behind.

In the search
for what is missing,
Found
is passed by.

Yet if you await
what time brings you,
Soul arrives.

## *plant new seeds*

The First planted seeds
sprout into being
then multiply
across the land.

Future generations
plant the same seeds
in the same way
cultivating the same story.

Until one day,
a young farmer
enriches the soil
to foster new growth.

Burrowing deep underground,
she touches the heart of creation
the lineage of the First seed.

As she forges past
the layers of the known,
Ancestors lead her through
the door of dark mystery

where vacant souls
are left unseen
and lost voices
remain unheard.

Amidst their tragic stories,
she finds strength
and the courage
to plant new seeds.

# *depth*

She is like a rare, fine wine

Don't expect
to open the bottle
and chug all at once

Expect to closely examine
her beautiful aura,
slowly take-in
her mysterious scent,
feel her texture
and swirl around in it
for a while

Take the time
to explore her origin,
know how her soul
has been tended
and what the harvest
has reaped

Indulge
in her complexity

Be prepared
at your first taste
to experience depth

*poetry*

My containment is strong
I feel its edges.

When my soul arrives
at the entrance,
I welcome her
I absorb her embrace.

Together,
we drink in the silence
until sound waves
recite poetry.

# fog's illusion

Fog used to be my shadow
now it is my gift

I bypass fog's illusion
to see alignment

No part of you
is left unseen

What is complete
departs

What is beginning
arrives

## *streaming*

The rising flame
burns bright
enticing me into stillness

I sink into earth's density
where the nourishment
of silence is found

In this realm,
ethereal beings
play music

My body enjoys
the streaming

# mind's way

I navigate the winding path
not knowing
what will be found

Making my way
through life's complexity
barely breathing

I sense the New World ahead
but detour
too many times

My soul speaks
as I stumble
on the difficult path I walk

But Mind
always gets its way

## the origin of you

Before your first breath
others were shaping
your life.

Their thoughts and actions
weaving your story,
the origin of you.

Whether you entered
a life of chaos or calm
you had no choice
but to endure.

Mind can't remember
your origin story
but your body
never forgets.

You are left
with the confusion
placed within you.

Yet you can return
to the beginning
to claim your pure heart.

Rewrite your story,
make each future step
your own.

*the new way*

Soul is ready to move ahead
but Mind stays behind
immersed in its old ways

It's all it knows
It hasn't experienced
what's yet to be told

The stop and start
of confusion,
the story of life
being taken apart

That is Mind's fear
not soul connection,
the new way
is presently in action

Beyond the mind,
Soul glides, it flies
it is destined
to arrive.

## *two views*

Two views always exist
you can choose one
or create your own mix.

Whatever way
you choose to go,
the other will try
to alter your flow.

Don't let other energies
muddy your clear water.

Stay true to yourself
and what you perceive,
within your containment
sustain soul purity.

Only your soul
has the right answer
and knows what's best
for your life.

Let all the rest
blow away
like dust in the wind

with no power
to take flight.

## soul direction

True North
charts the course
first to sky,
the moon, then star.

Soul descends
below the clouds.
Body ascends
to find direction.

In moon's cycle
through light and dark,
keep your sight
on the brightest star.

Aligned
between earth and sky,
soul direction
is clear.

## *love relationship*

I am immersed
in self-love
with my soul
with my body

In union with Spirit
In connection with Earth

I am immersed
in self-relationship
with my mind
my voice
my heart

I see her
I hear her
I know her
I trust her

This love relationship
rings clear

## evolved soul

I am a new soul.

I am a vulnerable infant
innocent child
serious girl
strong woman
aligned being.


*I hear this in reply:*


I am an evolved soul
made from earth
infused with star dust.

# NOVEMBER

## clear water

I stand
in the clear pool
of the Sacred

Sometimes,
I gently float
on the surface

Other times,
I dive
deep down

I swim
in its current

until the clear water
of the Sacred
becomes me

# *desire*

Your soul needs
only one thing,
Desire

The desire to
know who you are
be who you are,
to evolve
in this lifetime

Soul sits quietly
waiting
because it knows
without desire

words
crumble into dust

thoughts
rarely take flight

the flame of action
smolders
then quickly burns out

Soul needs desire
for the fruit of love
to ripen

*your words*

I

Words carry power,
are felt when spoken
or heard in-mind

They stream forth
with clarity
and pure intention,

or with carelessness
void of meaning
scattered
unable to land.

Wasted words
hover in midair
quick to evaporate.

Yet if spoken
with desire to hurt,

words fall
like stones
in a landslide
quick to bury
their victim.

## II

When others words
take aim with arrows
pointed at your heart,

let your wisdom
be the barricade
until they fall apart.

They are not yours
don't let them in.

Your words
are for you
to explore
feel
connect deeply
love.

# III

Words become the thread
to begin, to end
or untangle a story.

When gently carried
held close to heart,
they purify and enlighten.

Words carried
on wings of soul
take flight.

## shine bright

There are people in the world
who will do their best
to dim your light

They believe
if your light is extinguished,
they will shine brighter.

But contained light
cannot be altered
by external means

You determine
how brightly
you want to shine.

Bypass those
who attempt to place you
in their shadow

Instead, find people
who see your light
and want it to grow.

Most importantly,
be the lightkeeper

Take care of
your soul's inner light,
as it is destined
to shine bright.

## the flame

A wall of flame
is before you,
there is only one
way through

The flame contains
the wisdom
of your pain.

You can retreat
but eventually
you have to touch
your reality.

On the other side,
your heart
is waiting for you

to express
to feel
to know
to be real

The flame contains
what you need
to reclaim

your voice
your view
your strength
your gift

On the other side,
your soul
is waiting for you.

The flame contains
the essence
of your name.

## soul's seed

When your soul
speaks to you
it plants a seed

an opening
to enter the depths
touch grace
weed out the obstacles
you presently face

And if you reach into
the soil of soul
to cultivate a rich foundation

you will discover
profound ways
to grow love in your life

Soul's seed will reveal
the beautiful mystery
of You.

## *turned around*

At one point
on your journey
everything is turned around

What seemed happy
is now viewed as sad

What appeared dark
was actually light

What you thought
you knew, is not true

Your weakness, it turns out
is your greatest strength

So don't let your mind
take hold of you
and concretize your story

Instead, flow like water
change direction with wind
transform in fire

Let the stories that you tell
fall silent
as deep ground.

*invisible*

She blends into backgrounds
is barely seen in shadows
arrives unnoticed

Under her gray cloak
she drifts like thick fog
slowly merging into the landscape

A beautiful being
glimpsed one moment
gone the next
invisible

Her desire to be seen
vanishes midair
it fails to land.

Now,
being invisible
is her strength

She's the silent one
the observer
keenly aware
expertly bypassing
the obstacles

She moves into the shadows
to maneuver through chaos
untouched

She becomes fog
to bypass density

Amidst the reality
of humans' empty choices,
she doesn't want to be
seen in the crowd

She seeks
a new direction.

## soul's voice

Listen to the words
your mind wants to speak
either out loud
or heard within

Notice the ones
you want to hold on to.

Listen to the words
your body wants to speak
either in response
or thoughts of its own

Notice the ones
that cause you to feel.

Mind shares
past experience,
what it has learned

Body shares
present feelings,
what it needs

Now,
invite Soul's voice
into the conversation.

Joined together,
a greater perspective
deep understanding
and wisdom are held.

## sound to silence

Let universal harmony
be your background noise

while silence
is the ground
you stand on.

Let nature's music
be your love song

while silence
is the sky
you reach for.

Let your soul's voice
be the channel you tune into

while silence
is where
you dwell.

## not my story

I return to you
all of the words
you placed on me

words to harm
words unkind

none of them
came from my mind.

But as I stand
here and now
within my heart
the words resound

I carry their weight
as if it's my
dreadful fate.

I return to you
all of the words
you placed on me

words of worry
words of fear

this was not
my story to bear.

And now, they
are a part of me
I will reverse
this tragedy.

The words I hold
in mind, in heart
are mine to shape
or take apart.

The words I hold
align with me

they are my truth
my way
my destiny.

## *seen*

Come out of the shadows
to be seen
into the crystal clear
light of day

To follow river's stream
into the deep channel
of your dreams

And see the path
you strayed from long ago
when dark of night
absorbed your weary soul

Now that emptiness
has settled in,
your pure light
is seen once again

## *small hurts*

I

Each one
builds upon the other
until they become
a mountain
of small hurts

We carry them
on the surface
then bury them
deep inside

As they build,
the sting is felt
but the story
runs silent

Our pain
becomes our secret,
until we choose
to change it.

## II

When the origin
of your pain is known,
there is nothing to protect

One by one,
let each small hurt
be understood

Held close to heart,
the mountain
crumbles into dust

Flood with sorrow
until you cleanse
the earth.

# *broken words*

I

Erase all the words
you've ever said,
say goodbye
bury the dead.

Forget about
your carelessness,
the words you said
that snarled and hissed.

Buried underneath
the words we speak

We are afraid
We are hurt

We feel the need
to protect
our self-worth.

## II

Words can be voiced
to mask our fears,
defiantly
avoid our tears.

Or we can
quickly react,
using words
in harsh attack.

Words swiftly spoken
cover up what's wrong
and broken.

## III

We can use words
to dismiss, deflect,
deny and reject.

Or our words can heal
and speak directly
to the pain we feel.

Words have the power
to reclaim our worth
strengthen us
transform the hurt.

With awareness,
our words
can become
Whole.

## *your story*

Words become thoughts
thoughts become stories
stories create your way of being.

Before your words
take hold of you
pause, know their origin.

Are these your words
or the words that other people
have placed in your mind?

Don't let your story
be written
by someone else.

Instead,
let the words you say
reveal your truth inside.

Let deep relationship
with your thoughts
reflect how you feel.

Shape your story
so that what you speak
unveils self-love.

# *you and soul*

You
A shaped personality
formed body
created experience
one lifetime

An overlay of
human conditioning

Soul
An eternal essence
without form
evolving through experience
many lifetimes

Pure Being

Together
An amazing human

# *light and joy*

In the dark of night
and deep within
there is light

In the hollows of grief
in searing rage
there is joy

Light floods the dark
to expose
the unhealed

Joy aligns
with the love
you feel

Light contains Joy

## the web

Echoing voices
from longtime past
rise into awareness
to be freed at last.

I support my body
to move ahead
release the old
bury the dead.

I hear their story
feel their pain
I understand
why they remain.

A lineage web
connected within
from core to surface
it continues to spin.

I support my body
to move ahead
release the old
bury the dead.

I tell my story
feel my pain
I understand
why the web remains.

A lineage web
spirals within
from core to surface
it reverses its spin.

# *lost and found*

I

My body moves
in rhythm
with social conditioning

with eyes focused
on the potential gains
before me,

ears hearing
only the music
others play.

My hands grasp for
as many possessions
obtainable

while my mouth
seeks nourishment
to feed the emptiness.

I inhale the breath
of the collective,
but in the process
I have lost
Me.

II

I return to Me.

With eyes closed,
I listen to my breath
follow its pace.

I feel my heart beat
in synch with
breath's rhythm.

Thoughts
travel swiftly,
they alter my breath

until the quiet
settles in.

I breathe deeply,
my soul
nourishes me.

# *water being*

In the density of this body
made from earth,
I rise from ground
contained in a sphere of light

I am a water being
with an inner world
filled with life

I breathe into their lungs
I nourish their bodies
I protect them
from a harsh outer world.

I have been given
a small piece of earth
to care for.

## *within reach*

When you feel lost
overcome by sorrow,
reach for Earth's ground
to hold you close.

When despair sinks in
and captures your breath,
call on Spirit Wind
to clear the heaviness.

When your rage rises
rapidly bursts forth,
invite Earth's waters
to flow through you.

When fear takes hold
and freezes over,
reach for your soul
to light the way.

## vast space

Walk into the night
look up at the sky
see the vast space
before your eyes.

Stand in the ocean
look far and wide
absorb the view
beyond the tides.

Under your feet
far beyond sight
is the deep ground
fertile with life.

In the vast space
of body and soul,
for many lifetimes
truth is foretold.

## *carry me*

Within my mind,
I carry you.

Your story follows me
throughout my day,
the load is heavy.

When my mind is consumed
with thoughts of you
there is no space for me.

You are my friend,
but this does not mean
I will carry you.

In fact, maybe it's time
for you to carry me
for a while.

Sincerely,

The Earth

# ABOUT THE AUTHOR

I revel in my walk with soul, my body grounded to earth, with my sight on the moon. When I am not in dialogue with Spirit, writing, or guiding others you will find me in nature walking and listening. – Lana Lensman

www.ingramcontent.com/pod-product-compliance
Lightning Source LLC
Chambersburg PA
CBHW020421130626
46549CB00006B/2675